WHAT AM I?

Big, Rough, and Wrinkly

WHAT AM I?

By Moira Butterfield
Illustrated by Wayne Ford

RSVP
RAINTREE
STECK-VAUGHN
PUBLISHERS
The Steck-Vaughn Company

Austin, Texas

Published by Raintree Steck-Vaughn Publishers, an imprint of Steck-Vaughn Company

Editors: Jilly MacLeod, Kathy DeVico
Project Manager: Joyce Spicer
Electronic Production: Amy Atkinson
Designer: Helen James
Illustrator: Wayne Ford / Wildlife Art Agency

Library of Congress Cataloging-in-Publication Data

Butterfield, Moira, 1961-
    Big, rough, and wrinkly/by Moira Butterfield; illustrated by Wayne Ford.
    p.   cm. — (What am I?)
    Summary: A riddle asking the reader to guess which animal is being described precedes information about different parts of an elephant's body, how it behaves, and where it lives.
    ISBN 0-8172-4584-7
    1. African elephant — Juvenile literature.   [1. African elephant.   2. Elephants.]   I. Ford, Wayne, ill.   II. Title. III. Series.
    QL737.P98B88   1997
    599.6'1 — dc20   96-32109
                                                               CIP   AC

Printed in Portugal.
Bound in the United States.
1 2 3 4 5 6 7 8 9 0 LB 99 98 97 96

My ears are large.

I've got big feet.

I use my trunk to drink and eat.

My skin is wrinkly,

tough and gray.

I take a muddy bath each day.

What am I?

Here is my trunk.

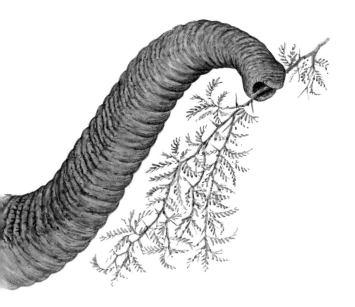

I use my trunk to pull leaves and twigs from the trees. Then I put them in my mouth. I eat nearly all day long.

Every day I bathe in the river. I use my trunk to drink the water. Sometimes I spray water onto my skin.

7

Here are my tusks.

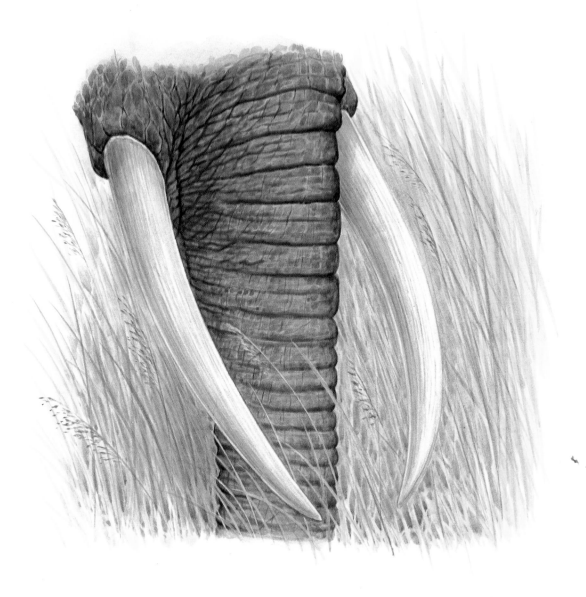

I have two tusks
that stick out from
my mouth. They are
long and sharp. I
use my tusks to tear
up grass to eat.

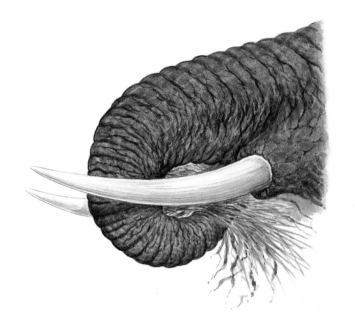

If something makes
me angry, I charge
at it with my tusks
sticking out. Look
how fast that lion
is running away!

Here is my ear.

I flap my big ears to keep myself cool. The place where I live is always very hot in the daytime.

When the sun feels too hot, I stand under some shady trees. How many birds can you find in the branches?

Here is my tail.

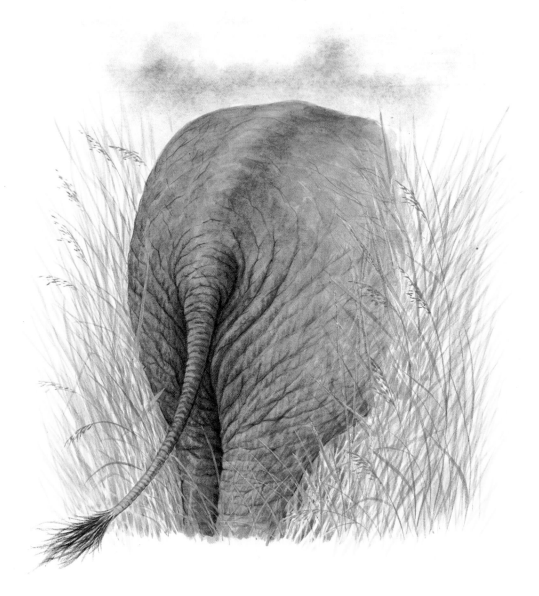

I swish it to keep away
the flies that buzz
around me all day
long. There are lots
of flies where I live.

Sometimes an egret
sits on my back and
pecks at the flies. I do
not mind giving the
egret a ride.

Here is my skin.

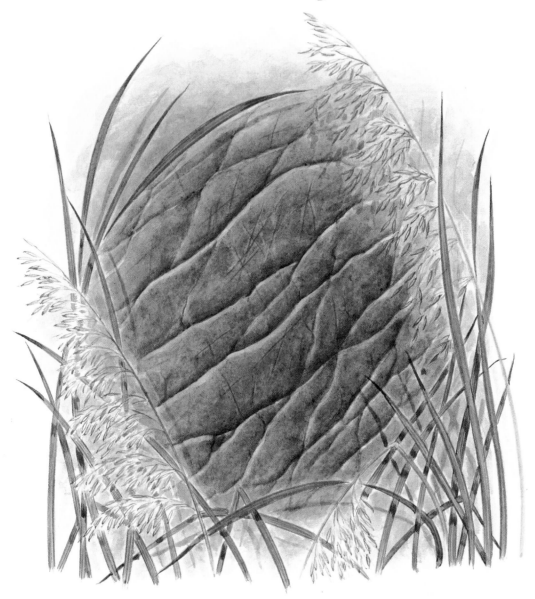

It is gray and wrinkly
and is about one
inch (3 cm) thick. I
like to sprinkle dust
on it to keep it soft.

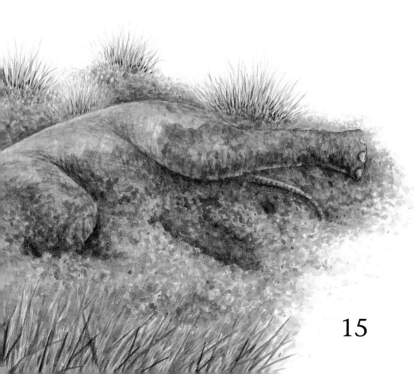

I love to roll in
slippery sloppy
mud. When I get
up, the mud dries
on me and helps
to keep me cool.

15

Here is my foot.

My feet are as
round and as wide
as tree trunks. My
whole body is very,
very big and heavy.

I can run and swim and
stand on my back feet
to reach up high.
Sometimes, I even
sleep standing up.

Here is my eye.

If I see something that frightens me
or makes me angry, I warn my friends.
I make a very loud noise.

I lift up my trunk and...
trumpet!
Have you guessed what I am?

I am an elephant.

Point to my...

big ears.

long trunk.

wrinkly skin.

four feet.

sharp tusks.

swishing tail.

I am called
an African
elephant.

21

Here is my baby.

She is called a calf.
I am her mother,
and I look after her.
We live with some
other elephants in
a herd.

Sometimes my calf
plays with the other
baby elephants.
They love to splash
around in the river.

Here is my home.

I live in grasslands.

Can you see me with my herd?
How many zebras, lions, giraffes,
and antelope can you find?

Here is a map of the world.

I live in a hot
land called Africa.
Where is it on
the map?

Can you point to the
place where you live?

Africa

Can you answer these questions about me?

What do I use my trunk for?

What do I like to eat?

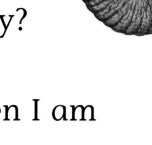

Where do I bathe every day?

What noise do I make when I am angry or frightened?

Why does the egret sit on my back?

What is my baby called?

What color is my skin?

Is my skin smooth like yours?

What do I do with my ears
to keep myself cool?

Here are words to help you learn about me.

calf The name for one of my babies.

grasslands The large grassy plains where I live with the rest of my herd.

herd The family of elephants I live with.

shady A cool place where there are shadows. I stand in a shady place when I want to keep out of the hot sun.

skin The thick gray covering over my body. You have skin, too. What is yours like?

sloppy Something that is runny and watery. The messy wet mud I like to roll in is sloppy.

trumpet The loud noise I make when I am scared or angry. Can you make a trumpeting noise, too?

trunk My long nose. I use it when I am eating and drinking.

tusks The long pointed teeth that stick out from my mouth.

wrinkly Something that has lots of creases and folds in it. My skin is wrinkly.